Minimalism

Achieve A Pristine And Well Ordered Living Space With
The Implementation Of Straightforward Minimalist
Cleaning Techniques And Do-it-yourself Shortcuts

*(A Pragmatic Minimalist Handbook On Techniques To
Streamline Your Household And Existence)*

Celeste Gouveia

TABLE OF CONTNET

Introduction To Minimalism 1

Strategies For Living A Better Life While Stress-Free 11

Form And Experiment 29

Creating Your Work 45

Moving On: Taking It Slow And Savoring Every Moment 78

The Effective Method For Organising Your Living Area 104

Evaluating Your Financial Condition 124

Getting Rid Of Your Inner Programming 143

Introduction To Minimalism

According to a quote from Jackie French Koller, one must either acquire a lot or have few desires to be wealthy. According to Tom Robbins, materialists are aware that what they possess truly possesses them. Having said that, minimalism is the way to go if you want to live a happy and fulfilling life. People have long practiced this manner of life. Since ancient times, philosophers, including the stoics, have recommended concentrating on spirituality and increasing wisdom rather than pursuing material wealth.

However, minimalism is more than owning a modest residence with a few pieces of furniture and a small wardrobe. You can use minimalism to break free from anxieties, guilt, despair, and the urge to measure your life to others. You can break free from the consumption culture that has shaped most people's lives.

What Is Minimalism Exactly?

To put it another way, minimalism is more about attitude than objects. Minimalist living aims to clear space for the things you cherish and eliminate anything that diverts your attention. You need to consider what you can take away or eliminate to increase your life's value. Remember that sometimes, little is more.

What Benefits Does Minimalism Offer?

You may reap so many advantages from minimalism. Here are a few of them:

Joy

You will be happy with what you have rather than feeling like you need more. You may appreciate what you already have and stop wanting more by practicing minimalism.

tranquility of mind

Your mind clears up when you worry less. You achieve mental clarity and tranquility. You even get rid of your failure-related concerns. You become less afraid of losing things when you own fewer of them. The fundamental tenet of minimalism is contentment with existing possessions.

Improved Health

Better health results from less stress. As you are aware, stress can lead to several illnesses, including hypertension, cancer, and heart disease.

Greater Room

Eliminating unnecessary items frees up space for the things you love. Psychological and material clutter: a messy home reflects a busy mind. When you eliminate the useless, you may also make more room for the people who genuinely care about and love you.

Greater Funds

The simplest explanation is this: if you purchase fewer items, you will spend less money overall, increasing your money. For most people, the biggest source of stress in their lives is insufficient money. You are wealthier than 25% of Americans if all you have is $10 and no debt. Give that some thought for a moment. People barely make ends meet to acquire items they don't need but nonetheless need to win over their peers. Life is full of surprises, and having financial control gives you a sense of worth surpassing the value of designer goods.

Extra Time

Another fundamental tenet of minimalism is that there is only one thing you never have more time. Take your time and pick your responsibilities wisely. Steer clear of accepting every invitation or request as much as you can. To free up more time for the people and things that matter in your life and yourself, learn how to say "no" to some things.

Sense of Objective

A higher feeling of purpose can be found when you deliberately choose to live with less when you choose a minimalist lifestyle. You have the option to discover your actual calling and experience true happiness, as opposed to immersing yourself in superficiality.

Increased Output

Productivity increases with fewer distractions and clutter. When your surroundings and thoughts are clear and organized, you can perform at your best at work. Instead of wasting time hunting for items, you can start working immediately. Clearer thinking can also occur when you are surrounded by order.

Reduced Comparative Analysis

You merely waste time and energy when comparing your life to others. Worse so, it keeps you from being content. You may feel you are missing out on some things when you compare. Becoming a Minimalist is letting go of financial prosperity comparisons with others and starting to have fewer desires.

Improved Bonds

When you eliminate the people and things that are extra from your life, you can improve your relationships with coworkers by increasing your efficiency at work. You can identify your true pals when you learn to live with less. Additionally, you will learn which of your relatives truly value you for who you are rather than what you own.

A more pristine environment

Minimalists use less materials. We live in a world where our shopping behavior directly affects our surroundings, but it's not just about money or the environment. In addition to being terrible for our wallets, fast fashion, disposable goods, and a throwaway culture also require that everything we discard find a home. Reducing one's usage contributes to a somewhat cleaner world.

Greater Command

Gaining more control over your life is the goal of becoming a Minimalist. Possessing too much stuff will simply heighten your materialistic cravings. Your material belongings and bank account will begin to control you instead of concentrating on the things that count, like your friends, family, and passions. The pursuit of wealth and material possessions will ultimately lead to a greater sense of isolation.

It will become simpler for you to tidy your wardrobe.
It is easier for you to clean up when you have fewer items. Everything is easy to locate, and you can swiftly return items to their proper locations. Additionally, you don't need to be concerned about losing anything.

It will become simpler for you to make selections.

It won't take long for you to get an instinctual sense of what to discard and preserve. You won't find that you need much when you start to consider what you truly need.

Strategies For Living A Better Life While Stress-Free

1: Awreness

Keep your eyes open, and don't let yourself become lost in your to-do lists. Eyes wide open, be "in your space." Your awareness shapes your capacity and decisions, so it's critical to carve out time and space to fully experience your experiences.

CHOICES PLUS AWARENESS = BETTER OUTCOMES. It also involves actively participating to give attention to the things, people, and places that bring you happiness. You can include more happy factors in place of the objects, people, or places that make you uncomfortable. Make your selections.

2: Presence

Beneath it all is that when we're stressed, our appearance changes. To choose not to submit to life's flow is called struggle. Be present in the moment. How much time do you take? It's more about realizing the moment and learning about not overcrowding your plate with tasks to complete. The secret is to live in "the now" of each given moment. What authenticity is all about is this movement towards experiencing.

It's about being present in your life's moments, not about rushing from one moment to the next or searching through what is happening. A common feeling among most of us is that something is missing. And that something is frequently you.

Time is a variable resource. Are you finding satisfaction in the way you use your time? Are you putting your life on display? Life exists just for the moment BEING (time to be).

3. Calm your thoughts

Discovering calmness in your days can lead to remarkable benefits such as enhanced clarity and concentration, reduced feelings of overwhelm, the ability to concentrate on what matters, weight loss, toned muscles, a general sense of ease and happiness, increased energy, and less emotional ups and downs.

4: Maintain a balanced emotional state

Simply put, emotions are feelings. The more we practice bringing emotions into balance rather than focusing solely on the positive or negative, the happier life becomes and the less stress we experience. You can find meaning in experiences by integrating them. That is when we can identify the emotion and choose to act rather than react. The benefit is that it allows you to be who you are. We tend to suppress our emotions until we are prepared to face reality.

5: Adhere to your values

The most inspiring thing is also the most valuable to you. Living up to your highest ideals will make you feel inspired, meaningful, and purposeful. Spend no more time living in a place that doesn't feel important to you. Your values define your life. Decide what matters most, then live from that space. Everything less is less, and that equals tension.

How to Get Rid of an RV

1. To begin with, it helps to identify what exactly you are envious of. What is it that you would like to have for yourself?

2. Take a step back and determine whether you already have some manifestation in your life. Frequently, what we observe in others is just a mirror of something within ourselves.

3. Ask yourself, how can I, or how can I benefit from this person's actions or being? How do I make this into something that tastes good?

4. Ask yourself: How can you find a place of grace and let go of your envy?

When you give in to envy, can you still find happiness and love?

It's difficult to imagine living in a world where everyone is perched on the peaks of inequity and not noticing that our pedestal was or maybe a little bit lower. It's simple to comprehend that jealousy is not a productive thought or emotion.

After all, being an environment never becomes your pedestal because it must be created, but it's difficult not to desire what others possess. However, the text appears to be one of the most practical challenges since it requires us to choose to give up jealousy to achieve the best form of love and pleasure.

HOODNEss. Acquiring love and happiness is not a simple task.

How to Let Go of Struggles

Not only is learning how to release stress easier than learning how to increase brain power, but you can learn how to do both at the same time. This is a long-term plan that represents a lifestyle transformation for many. If you work long hours daily or are a couch potato, this may seem daunting. The returns are excellent.

Making your program more resilient, delaying aging, and understanding how to cope with stress will mean that you won't need to make as many severe or unexpected changes to your way of life as you get older.

Realize that you may prevent early aging, stress-related illnesses, and physical and mental deterioration. As you age, you can also benefit from improved moods and critical thinking abilities.

Why and How to Maintain a Clean Haven?

It sounds appealing to live in a clutter-free, spotless home. Living a clutter-free life is also my ideal concept. However, we frequently unwind and let our haven become disorganized and messy. Living in a clean and organized home has many benefits, such as less mess, better hygiene, lower debt, improved home organization, and a stress-free existence. But if your house appears to be a haven for mess, clutter, and complete disarray, you could quickly get so overwhelmed that you give up on maintaining a tidy home. Does that imply that after weeks or even months of desertion, you should live in all the trash your house becomes?

Naturally, no. You are aware that you cannot continue living in a dirty home. If this is the case, you ought to combat the sloth that presumably leaves you unsure where to begin.

Yes, it will likely be difficult and stressful to declutter a house that hasn't been done in weeks or even months, but the good news is that every step you take will bring your home closer to being tidy. Organizing your home may be enjoyable, particularly if you approach it enthusiastically and creatively. How, then, should you approach it? Here are some pointers for maintaining a clean and clutter-free house.

#1 One by one

Focus on one task at a time and do it thoroughly. Taking on too much at once will make you easily tired and disinterested. # 2 Trash bag trick: Start in any area, but focus especially on the one that requires immediate attention.

Grab a medium-sized trash bag and begin stuffing it full of random items you find lying around. Find out how quickly you can fill it. You'll soon have a bag full of useless items that you may get rid of to make your house cleaner.

#3 Vacuuming the closet

Your wardrobe may be a terrific place to plunder and find a lot of outfits you never intended to wear. Decide which clothes you wear most frequently. Sort them out from the people who usually hang out and never even receive a look from you. Throw these garments away or even donate them. Use the same method to empty any closets in your house that might store toys, books, linens, or other items. Give away any books you may have stored in your wardrobe.

#4 The 12/12/12 con

Determine which 12 items need disposal, which 12 can be donated to charitable organizations, and which 12 have been moved from their original location. This is a creative and entertaining method to arrange your area. Using this approach, you can engage your family and observe how engaging the cleaning activity becomes.

#5 Original viewpoints

If you have the "I-May-Need-It" condition, you should treat your viewpoint first. You hoard everything for a very long time when you have this dangerous disorder. You should have a clear head and begin decluttering originally. Utilise goods with multiple uses, then get rid of those whose tasks have already been fulfilled by them. If you find something too tough to get rid of, consider how much more room it would provide in your house.

#6: The Four Baskets Method

Obtain four enormous buckets and mark them Trash, Keep, Donate, and Retain to simplify cleaning. Sort items in your house according to their purposes, paying particular attention to the storage area. Don't ignore any space in the room; give each object careful thought. It might take a few days or weeks to complete, but the effort would be worthwhile.

Five Minute Power

You may divide the time you spend on different chores into 5-minute assignments because clearing out large amounts of debris over extended periods is tiresome and monotonous. I believe spending five minutes completing easy housekeeping tasks won't overwhelm you. If you set aside five minutes each day, both in the morning and the evening, to clean, just imagine how much you will have accomplished in a week or even a month. Even if you accomplished something, would you even know it?

*Deal with the papers that are floating.

Clutter is largely composed of official documents and newspapers. Put them where they belong in five minutes. Put them in a tray with all the floating papers if they don't already have a dedicated spot. The living room should only have current newspapers; all previous issues should be carefully piled until they are taken to a scrap dealer. Additionally, arrange documents such as manuals, brochures, posters, booklets, receipts, and announcements according to their proper categories. Establish a daily zero-clutter zone.

Imagine an area that is clutter-free and devoid of any kind of mess. Commence at any desired location. It could be anything like a bedside table, dining table, study table, or kitchen counter. Just be careful that nothing that isn't in use is put in that area. Now extend the perimeter of zero clutter. Your family will designate your house as a "zero-clutter home" in a few days.

*Take up a shelf

Clear out a shelf every day and return everything to its proper place. It can be a shelf in your kitchen cabinet or your wardrobe in your bedroom.

* Coincidence 5

Place the five items you choose at random in their proper locations.

Moving items neatly piled in one location by picking them up is inappropriate. Look for items that have been moved after being used. Items like towels, shoes, newspapers, magazines, pens, and notepads are likely misplaced.

* Illustration

Simply close your eyes and picture the type of space you desire. This will provide a framework to organize the room more effectively and logically. You can tell from your visualization what you should and shouldn't keep.

*Create a "maybe" box.

Take a "perhaps" labeled cardboard box or basket. Go through your house and arrange everything that doesn't appear important but might be useful later in the next five minutes. This box will hold everything that can't be thrown away right away. Continue taking 5-minute rounds with this box, and when it's full, store it in your storehouse or garage. After three months, remove the box and decide what should be thrown away and what can be kept.

*Take off any unnecessary clothing.

Take everything from your wardrobe you haven't worn in the last month. If you put in five minutes for this exercise, your wardrobe will soon be less than it was five minutes ago.

Form And Experiment

The foundation of creativity, despite its appearance of mystery and complexity, is really basic. In addition to other accomplishments, Herbert Simon, a cognitive scientist and software engineer who won the Nobel Prize, is credited with creating the term "artificial intelligence." He asserts that the two main activities of creative individuals are coming up with a lengthy list of ideas within and related to their field and evaluating those ideas against the demands of the problem and the actual reality. In other words, "Generate and Test" is the essence of creativity, according to Simon.

Is this all there is to it? The explanation of the method makes it appear straightforward, but the complexity and difficulties come with how it is carried out. Examining these procedures can help solve the puzzle of how such a basic model of creativity can provide creators trying to create new things with incredible outcomes.

As we've seen in other parts of the book, Edison is renowned for developing novel ideas practically daily. Over his 84 years, Edison filed an astounding 1093 patent applications. Based on the assumption that a successful patent would have at least ten failed ideas, Edison would have developed 10930 ideas in his lifetime, or one idea every three days. These concepts emerged from various fields, and many were implemented in people's daily lives. Some of these concepts, such as the phonograph, light bulb, movie camera, telephone, and telegraph, altered the course of human history. We tend to overlook Edison's many failures, such as the talking dolls, the use of sound in motion pictures, and the construction of pianos out of cement. He took great pleasure in developing fresh concepts that might turn into profitable products. In addition, he developed prototypes and introduced several items, many of which were commercial failures.

What can we learn from the successful generation and testing of new ideas by individuals like Edison?

THEY DO NOT CARE THAT THEY FAIL.

Edison was a tireless inventor who never stopped developing concepts that might not succeed. Fear of not succeeding is one of the things that keepscreatives locked on novel concepts. Failure is crippling and robs artists of the energy needed to produce fresh concepts. Failures fuel effective inventors, and they use that energy to come up with new ideas. Failure is more prevalent than success in the creative industries, as everyone involved in the area knows, and the ability to draw energy from failure is a crucial success factor in the creative domains.

THEY WORK IN VARIOUS AREAS

A phenomenon known as "Creative Block" is familiar to anyone who has pursued a career in the creative industry. When forced to develop fresh concepts for a novel, characters, or storyline, writers experience writer's block. It is also a typical experience for business owners. Being interested in numerous, diverse fields with few elements in common is one of the primary factors that help them. They simply switch gears and practice the other field when they get stuck. During his Nobel Prize-winning research on the decision-making processes of administrators, Herbert Simon encountered a problem with the differential equation simulation. He began utilizing a newly emerging field, computers, and went on to found artificial intelligence. He eventually won the Nobel Prize in economics for his views on human decision-making derived from his computer tests.

THEY ARE WELL-INFORMED ON DOMAINS

Upon his return from vacation, Alexander Fleming discovered fungus growing on the Petri plate containing the bacteria he had preserved for future study. It dawned on him that the fungus was keeping the germs from proliferating. This coincidental encounter spurred him to do more study, and in the end, he created Penicillin, which revolutionized the treatment of bacterial diseases. Dr. Fleming would not have recognized the impact of fungus on bacteria if he had not had extensive knowledge of bacterial infection. People with deep domain expertise and effective Generate and Test cycle mastery are responsible for many inventions. Testing a concept in a real-world setting is crucial to ensure that it makes sense and has a practical application, especially in fields like design, crafts, and entrepreneurship, where effective creativity is largely dependent on real-world manifestation.

Chapter 2: The Entire Wellbeing Advantages of Minimalism

With good reason, minimalism has become a popular term in recent years! Numerous individuals who have adopted a minimalist and simple lifestyle assert that it has had a major positive impact on their general wellbeing. In this chapter, we'll talk about minimalism's advantages for your life.

1. Less Stress

Stress reduction is one of minimalism's most important advantages. This leads to tension and anxiety, which can then show up in a lot of other areas of your life. Simplifying your living area and belongings can help create a more tranquil space that eases tension and encourages relaxation.

2. Enhanced Contentment

By concentrating on the things that are most important to you, minimalism can make you happier. By simplifying your life, you can eliminate distractions and concentrate on the things that make you happy and fulfilled. Overall happiness and a more meaningful existence may result from this.

3. Greater Length and Autonomy

Eliminating the need to continuously clean, arrange, and care for many items will also free up more time for you. You may free up time and energy to do the things you enjoy most by simplifying your life.

4. Better Connections

The improvement of relationships is another advantage of minimalism. By simplifying your life, you can concentrate more on the people in your life and less on material belongings. Doing this may result in deeper and more meaningful relationships with people around you.

5. Enhanced Concentration and Output

Eliminating distractions and concentrating on what matters might help you become more focused and productive. By streamlining your life, you may establish a clutter-free space that encourages focus and productivity.

6. Better Cash Situation

As minimalism helps reduce wasteful spending and save money, it can also improve your financial situation. You may save money for experiences and pursuits that make you happy and fulfilled by simplifying your life and minimizing the amount of belongings you own.

7. Better Health

Finally, minimalism can benefit your health by lowering stress levels, encouraging relaxation, and enhancing sleep. Your life can be simpler, leading to a calmer atmosphere and better health results.

To sum up, there are a lot of wide-ranging advantages to minimalism. You may design a more tranquil and fulfilling life that provides joy, happiness, and fulfillment by emphasizing simplicity and eliminating distractions. Whether your objectives are to boost productivity, lower stress levels, or enhance your general well-being, minimalism is important.

Chapter 1: Why We Accumulate and the Psychology of Clutter

Many of us battle clutter, but knowing the psychology of it can help us better understand why we accumulate it and how to deal with it. This chapter will examine the causes of clutter buildup, how it affects our physical and mental health, and how to stop the accumulation cycle.

The fact that clutter can be connected to our feelings is one of the primary reasons we gather it. Because of its sentimental worth, clutter can act as a reminder of past events or memories, making it difficult to go with them. Clutter can also be an attempt to hang onto something that we believe will be valuable or useful. For example, we might save a pile of magazines that we want to read sometime or hang onto clothing that we hope to fit into again.

Clutter can also indicate procrastination, so we like to amass it. Whether it's because we don't want to take the time to go through our belongings or the reality of parting with something, we may put off making decisions regarding them.

Having too much stuff around might make it difficult to stay organized, and clutter can also indicate disorganization.

Trying to keep track of everything we own and locate what we need when we need them.

Clutter can have a big impact on our physical and emotional health. Not only may clutter impair our ability to focus and be productive, but it can also exacerbate emotions of tension, anxiety, and despair. It may also make it challenging to unwind and take in our surroundings. Because it can be challenging to clean and maintain our living spaces, clutter can also harm our physical health.

Although it can be difficult, breaking the cycle of accumulating is achievable. The next chapters of this book will teach you how to break that loop.

In conclusion, the first step to ending the cycle of accumulation is realizing the psychology underlying clutter and the reasons behind our collection of it. This chapter sheds light on clutter accumulation's psychological and emotional causes and how it impacts our physical and mental health.

In the upcoming chapter, we will look at how minimalism can enhance our physical and mental wellbeing, including lowering stress, encouraging relaxation, and boosting productivity.

12) Look for Inspiration: Read books or subscribe to podcasts and blogs about minimalism to get ideas from other minimalists.

Creating Your Work

Locating freelance or remote employment options.

In the digital age, finding remote employment or freelance possibilities is becoming easier because of the abundance of platforms and tools available. This comprehensive handbook will help you land that dream job or project.

Start by looking at internet employment boards. Many of them concentrate on freelancing and remote work. There are niche job boards that target particular skills, general freelance platforms where you may bid on tasks, and job boards specifically for remote work.

Developing a network is essential. Make sure to emphasize on your LinkedIn profile that you are interested in freelance or remote work. Check here often for job openings. Alumni networks and social media are excellent resources for finding possibilities.

Sometimes, going straight ahead is the best course of action. Send cold emails to businesses you respect or apply to work for them. Taking the initiative can frequently result in unanticipated opportunities.

Take notice of the influence that remote work communities and digital nomads have. Slack channels, online communities, and forums are not only great places to have conversations but also great places to find employment openings.

Websites that aggregate jobs are your one-stop source for a variety of postings. You may filter especially for remote roles on websites like Indeed and Glassdoor, which provide many chances.

Even abroad, co-working facilities can be a veritable treasure for networking. Participate in their classes, mixers, and events; you never know who you'll run into or what chances may present themselves.

Maintaining your competitive edge in the remote work market requires regular skill upgrades. Obtaining credentials in your field and taking online courses can greatly increase your employability.

Last but not least, you can stand out with a strong portfolio and a CV that is customized for remote work. Ensure it features your greatest work, whether an online portfolio or a separate website. Finding secure remote employment may take more initiative and persistence than looking for a job traditionally, but the freedom and flexibility are worthwhile. Persist, continue honing your craft, and engage in active networking.

The art of no: Selecting endeavors in line with your principles.

Your projects must reflect your ideals and way of life, particularly if you lead a minimalist or digital nomad lifestyle. It all comes down to identifying the ideal balance between your values and aspirations for your lifestyle and work life.

Take some time to ponder about yourself. Which fundamental beliefs guide you? It might be innovation, work-life balance, or environmental sustainability. Describe the lifestyle you want to lead. If you're a digital nomad, you probably seek remote job choices and flexible tasks. Establish boundaries regarding your work hours, the kinds of activities you're ready to take on, and the industries or practices you desire to stay away from.

Think about how the project fits with your values when assessing possible initiatives. Do you share the same values as the client's mission? Think about the workplace also: does it provide you with the required freedom and balance? Seek for initiatives that present growth prospects and ensure the pay is equitable.

It takes skill to turn down tasks that don't fit your principles. Express gratitude and, honestly but kindly, explain that you are concentrating on projects that better align with your values or way of life. Referencing others for the project can benefit the client and promote goodwill. Always reply quickly and keep an eye out for chances that may arise in the future that would be a better fit.

Review your values and objectives regularly. Your priorities will change as you do. When you look back on your endeavors, do they reflect your values? This input will greatly influence future decisions.

You will gradually establish a reputation in your niche by continuously selecting jobs that align with your ideals. This draws in similar projects and clients. Making connections in groups that align with your principles is also essential.

Recall that while taking on any project—especially profitable ones—may seem appealing, putting your principles and lifestyle first will result in more success and fulfillment in the long run. It sustains your drive, enthusiasm, and dedication to your work.

Juggling work and life while traveling.

However, maintaining that balance is necessary for long-term performance, productivity, and well-being.

Here's how to handle it without going too far in either direction with yourself.

Set up boundaries first. Having a distinct workstation is crucial, even for nomads. This aids in mentally separating work from play. Establish digital "do not disturb" hours to show respect for your time and stick to defined work hours.

Burnout can be avoided by planning frequent breaks. Use methods such as the Pomodoro technique, which involves working 25 minutes and taking 5 minutes off. Ensure you unplug and recharge for a longer period, at least once a day.

Setting work priorities is essential. Sort your to-do list by priority and due date before you begin your workday or workweek. Use technology with task management tools such as Asana or Trello.

Acquire delegation skills. Concentrate on your strongest skills and think about outsourcing the rest. Never be afraid to ask for assistance, whether you're working with freelancers or employing a virtual assistant.

Have reasonable expectations for yourself. Saying no or requesting an extension is OK. Make sure you're not overworking yourself by periodically evaluating your workload.

Allocate time for personal pursuits. To reduce stress and stay focused, engage in hobbies, physical activity, and meditation.

Give clients or coworkers clear notice of your availability. Establish expectations for your response times, particularly after hours.

It's critical to regularly unplug. Make time for regular vacations, even if only staycations, and set aside time for a digital detox. The intention is to be completely cut off from employment.

Ask for and receive feedback on your work habits from others and yourself.

This may offer insightful information for advancement.

Lastly, never forget why you began this trip. Review your objectives frequently and acknowledge your minor successes. This keeps you engaged and helps you reorient your efforts.

As a digital nomad, finding work-life balance requires deliberate effort, introspection, and flexibility in response to changing circumstances and demands. Working within yourself, not against yourself, is possible if you set clear boundaries and pay attention to your well-being.

Introduction: What Is Stress?

What about a couple of chocolate chip cookies? Is it so stressful? If you include two chocolate chip cookies in a well-balanced daily diet, nothing at all. Plenty, consume the full bag of double fudge chocolate chunks if you abstain from desserts for a month. You're not used to having so many cookies. That much sugar isn't accustomed to your body. That is a source of tension. It's difficult but not as stressful as totaling your car or getting sent to Siberia.

The American Institute of Stress, located in Yonkers, New York, reports that between 75 and 90 complaints or disorders connected to stress, and 43 percent of adult patients have negative health impacts as a result of stress.

Likewise, your body experiences stress from anything abnormal for you. That tension feels fantastic in parts. Excellent even. Life would be quite dull if there was no tension at all. Although stress isn't inherently evil, it's also not necessarily beneficial. It may seriously harm your health if it occurs too frequently or for too long.

But stress isn't limited to unusual situations. Additionally, stress might be well-hidden and ingrained in your life. What if you detest your middle management position but still show up for work every day out of fear of quitting and losing your steady income? What happens if there are major communication issues in your family or if you don't feel comfortable where you live? Even when everything appears to be good, you may be dissatisfied. Things like unclean dishes in the sink, unsupportive family members, and twelve-hour workdays at the office can cause tension even if you're used to them. When something goes well, you may even become anxious. Perhaps when someone is friendly, you start to get suspicious, or if your home is excessively tidy, it makes you uneasy. You don't know how to adjust because you're accustomed to challenging things. Stress is a peculiar and very personal experience.

You've undoubtedly heard a lot about stress in the media, at the coffee maker at work, or in the periodicals and newspapers you read, unless you live in a cave without television—which is not a bad method to reduce stress. Most people have preconceived ideas about what stress means to them and what it is in general. For you, what does stress mean?

- Unease?
- Pain?
- Concern?
- Fear?
- Joy?
- Fear?
- Lack of certainty?

These factors stress people out and are primarily stress-related ailments. However, what is stress? The term "stress" may appear ill-defined since it encompasses so many distinct types of stress that affect many people in many different ways. To one person, something might be thrilling and worrisome. What precisely is stress, then?

Let's examine each type of stress and its effects on you in more detail.

Stress Reduction for Your Spirit and Mind

The mind's capacity to fend off the damaging effects of stress will be strengthened by stress management strategies that fortify and strengthen the body. However, other stress-reduction strategies focus specifically on the mind, including thought patterns, feelings, intelligence, and, beyond the mind, the search for spiritual purpose. The best methods for addressing your mind and spirit are those found in this chapter, which will focus on meditation.

Stress's Harmful Effects on the Mind

One's incapacity to focus

- Uncontrollably excessive worry
- Panic and anxious feelings
- Ignorance
- Depression and sadness
- Unease
- Tiredness and poor energy
- Sensitivity
- Anxiety
- Negativism
- Fear
- Impractical anticipations
- Hopelessness

While it's true that certain stress-related symptoms have a direct physical cause, these symptoms are frequently the result of how the mind interprets, obsesses over, or becomes attached to stressful situations. How can one mentally prepare for stress? Naturally, with mental stress management.

The goal of stress management for the mind and spirit is to aid people suffering stress that exceeds their threshold for stress by stilling, calming, and quieting their busy minds. With these strategies, you can become aware of the attitudes that can set off a stress reaction, the thought patterns that make you feel more stressed, and the ways in which you tend to hold onto thoughts like they are life preservers. They can also satisfy the need for a deeper purpose that, when unfulfilled by a life that doesn't live up to our expectations, can gradually sap our happiness and self-worth.

Because the mind and body are intertwined, some strategies are physical stress management procedures (relaxation techniques). However, if you feel the need to address your spirit directly and are suffering some of the negative mental impacts of stress, try these stress management strategies for mind and spirit.

What Does Minimalism Involve?

1) Describe the thing.

We can summarize the information in the introduction by saying that minimalism is a way of living. It's a method of leading a meaningful life supported by the necessities of daily existence. A minimalist will only retain objects in their houses, minds, and lives that are meaningful and purposeful. However, each person's choice is unique and based on their needs and preferences. For instance, the guitar you have hanging on your wall may or may not be minimalist. Whether or not it benefits you is the determining factor.

Based on my personal experience, I have to admit that I never became a minimalist. Rather, I recently realized that I am one. Although I like shopping, I never felt the need to purchase items needlessly. I never participated in sales promotions, purchased things in quantity, etc. You may find yourself in a similar circumstance. You lead a simple life. All you have to do is acknowledge this, and perhaps after reading this book, get better at being minimalist.

If none of the above describes you, you might be looking for advice on adopting a minimalist lifestyle. You will discover hints in this book about how to live a more minimalist lifestyle, but the change originates internally, not externally. You have to identify as a minimalist. Prepare to eliminate the things you recognize are superfluous and envision your life free of them. It should be something yelling from your spirit, not an attempt to fit in with the latest fashion.

Minimalism and other housekeeping and lifestyle habits like decluttering and tidying up are sometimes confused. It's not entirely incorrect that people frequently lump all three under the same discussion topic. Although these practices differ greatly, they are all intimately related. What, then, is shared by them?

Well, decluttering and tidying up mainly focus on rearrangement of your space, but minimalism focuses on having a conscious relationship with everything around you. These are habits to maintain a tidy and orderly living space, thoughts, and existence. However, they might also serve to achieve or sustain a minimalist lifestyle. Thus, the intimate relationship.

For instance, a minimalist will need to tidy and organize their home in their unique style to have a better relationship with the items inside. Put another way, maintaining the essence and significance of your life will require additional routines like cleaning and organizing. "Your way" will be the process's essential phrase, and I'll explain why.

Since every person is unique, so are their needs. Many pieces of hardware could be removed from the garage of a minimalist writer. However, a minimalist carpenter will have a large toolkit since these are necessities. Furthermore, you can still identify as a minimalist if you use tools as a hobby rather than for employment.

Living a minimalist lifestyle is a personal decision. Different perspectives on how to apply it to one's life would only make sense. Some people have a minimalist approach to owning and maintaining material possessions, while others consider mental clutter-clearing a minimalist requirement.

There are many different types of minimalism available if you search online. Countless YouTube videos exist from which you might construct your definition of a minimalist existence. In Facebook communities for minimalists, you can also make friends. Just keep in mind to exercise selectivity and avoid becoming paralyzed by the abundance of possibilities available. Minimizing can, after all, also be applied to your interactions on social media.

Being minimalist is a deliberate life path rather than an objective. The end is not in sight. It is an ongoing process of self-change, a steady alteration of behaviors. You can preserve your life's essentiality and purpose by practicing minimalism.

Eliminating the Superfluous

In the kitchen, we have an abundance of useless items. What percentage of the equipment do you have to have that is used on a regular basis? Find cabinet space for your food processor and toaster if they are taking up counter space and you don't use them more than once or twice a week. They have a much more streamlined appearance. The lack of cabinet space could be an issue that has to be fixed. How frequently will you need all those plates for a dinner party? Sort through your cabinets and save only the necessities. You can keep your dinnerware for Thanksgiving and other festivities in your basement or attic.

Anything you wouldn't use to clean yourself shouldn't be in your bathroom. Things that are merely for decoration in the bathroom only harbor bacteria. Some of those big box retailers tell us that to create a spa-like atmosphere in our bathrooms, we need rubber ducky shower rings, coordinating trash cans, unique rugs, and decorations—things that are not necessary. Make your bathroom appear as though it is a very functioning space. Recall that using a single wipe with an antibacterial cleaner will make cleaning much easier than getting into all the little crevices and nooks.

Like the entrance in the last chapter, your office tells a whole new tale. Simplify the process by monitoring what you retain and discard. If you only use one pen at a time, don't buy 200. Even while the large package of highlighters seems like a fantastic value, what good is it if you have to keep them in storage until they get too dry to use?

Easygoing

Simplicity is challenging in these settings since we need a lot of our "stuff." Your kitchen will be the largest alteration you make here. Buying in bulk or stocking up on food items during sales is popular among consumers. That isn't the ideal approach if you want to keep things simple and organized. For one week, concentrate on purchasing the necessities for your family, and then begin anew the next week in addition to reducing the amount of food you toss out, which will free up more of your storage for other items. This is also a fantastic approach to start eating healthier because most of the bulk-purchased, highly space-consuming goods we buy are processed foods that we shouldn't be eating in the first place. Try to keep your bathroom inventory to a minimum. This does not include purchasing multipurpose cleaning products that clean your body, hair, and automobile. Rather, it refers to using up a product completely before buying more.

The same rule applies to buying bathroom supplies: avoid buying too much in bulk as this will need storing everything you purchase. Buy what you need instead. You should throw away any goods that you find that you don't particularly enjoy. We frequently believe that we should keep anything we purchase until they are used up. But you won't use it very often, so ultimately, it will just go bad.

Pay attention to what you need for your office. Generally speaking, if you need a room in your house that escapes the rules of minimalism, your office is the best option. Your home office should be used exclusively for work-related purposes; you cannot keep items from other house rooms. Avoid combining two different sorts of spaces in your office; having an office that also serves as a fitness room is a surefire way to run into problems.

Concentrate

The kitchen island, table, and counter areas should be focal points. Ensure that they are as empty as possible. To make cleaning easier, install one of those hanging racks if you don't have enough room for your pots and pans. Mason jars are another popular organizer for cabinets among many individuals. You can take those mason jars to the grocery store and fill them with dry items. This will not only benefit simplicity and your organization but also save you money and protect the environment. It's a given that every home has a "junk drawer," therefore you should also be careful to get rid of it. Even while a rubbish drawer alone isn't a concern, everyone in the home is. When there's just one place to chuck it all, we can't resist!

Under-sink storage is a must in your bathroom, or you may buy bath caddies (the kind you most likely used in college) for every family member. You may then coordinate the colors of the bath caddy with the other items utilized, such as a washcloth, soap dish, and bath products, to simplify things.

To aid with focus, you should set up a routine in your home office. Keep everything tidy and orderly by using bins and baskets. Invest in a filing system to keep your paperwork organized and off your desk. All these will help you feel more motivated to work and reduce the stress of working from home. Working from home appeals to those who truly wish to lead a minimalist lifestyle because it may even remove the need for a car and clothes tailored for the workplace.

Cut off

The strategy is the same as in the last chapter: eliminate the technologies you don't utilize. Technology causes mental clutter in addition to clutter in your house. Take out any radios and televisions from the kitchen. It is smaller than a regular radio and can be useful if you enjoy singing in the shower.

It can be different in your home office because you'll require technology. On the other hand, a radio, microwave, typewriter, calculator, television, or typewriter are not necessary. Everything you have in another room or on your computer.

Moving On: Taking It Slow AndSavoring Every Moment

The idea of minimalism is predicated on eliminating waste, as was previously said. We are urged to participate in as many clubs as possible at school to maximize our educational opportunities. We are supposed to be more responsible and productive at work. We come across never-ending to-do lists even at home. Even if a large number of individuals are unhappy and use medication to manage their stress and depression, we nevertheless live as though there is nothing wrong with this system. Our minds have been muddled by all of these burdens, leaving us with a persistent and overwhelming feeling that there is something we should have done but forgot. When we truly take the time to do nothing, see a worm scuttling over the pavement, or indulge in laziness with friends, we frequently feel bad about it. There's no feeling of rest or fulfillment.

Finding a cause to be happy is difficult when these feelings are eating away from us. It doesn't have to be this way in life. When you slow down and accept the alternative, everything becomes calm again. It is essential to slow down, particularly when we begin to feel that napping is a sign of sloth or when our internet connection is too slow to use.

The concern that something horrible would happen if things don't get done can make it challenging to break free from our ingrained routines and thinking and disconnect from the life we know. We put in more effort and longer work hours to ease that worry, only to find that there is never enough time. When the grind wears you out, take a step back, evaluate what matters, and concentrate your efforts on that. Releasing yourself from the need to accomplish everything can lead to an incredibly freeing high.

Here are some strategies for escaping the rat race if you want to live a simple "life in the slow lane":

*Select three daily tasks to complete: It's simple to think of a hundred things you should get done each day but resist the urge to do so. Reducing the size of your list will compel you to decide what matters most. After finishing the list, take the remainder of the day off to unwind and celebrate your accomplishments. This strategy will guarantee that you finish 21 chores each week.

* Develop your "no" skills: Quit taking on more than you can manage. For instance, volunteering is a wonderful way to spend your time, but if you put too much effort into it, you risk losing your happiness and the reason behind volunteering.

*Be ineffective: Set aside at least twenty minutes daily to engage in ineffectiveness. Don't read anything to advance your job or do anything to please your pals. Try something ridiculous and seemingly insignificant, like skipping rocks across a pond or creating mud pies with your children.

*Only check your social media accounts twice daily: Steer clear of constantly monitoring your email, Twitter, Facebook, stocks, blogs, sports scores, and other social media platforms. Using these websites can lead to addiction and rob you of time that could be spent on activities that genuinely bring you joy.

* Prioritise quality above quantity. Choose the organizations that truly improve your life rather than joining everyone accessible to you. Select three or four blogs and pay close attention to them. Locate a group that is doing work

you are passionate about and provide your support to them. Selecting quality over quantity will improve your overall satisfaction and reduce stress in your life.

*Create a hobby: Give a novel activity a try. Don't stress over being proficient at it. Rather, use your imagination and your passions. Yoga, jogging, rock climbing, reading, surfing, woodworking, painting, gardening, blogging, and woodworking are all excellent examples.

*Make time for the people you care about. If you only remember one thing from this section, it should be to spend time with the people you love. The foundation of a life with meaning is a relationship. To slow down and enjoy life, there's nothing better than to share secrets, dreams, and anxieties with another human. Lack of personal interaction with people might lead to a solitary and icy attitude toward life.

Chapter 1: Essentials of a Minimalist Budget: Developing a Minimalist Mentality

What is and is not a minimalist budget

A minimalist budget may seem like an extreme version of economic spending to many. They see someone collecting coupons all day, eating canned goods, and sleeping on a floor mattress. Being thrifty and having a minimalist budget are two entirely different things.

A minimalist budget focuses on organizing your money, setting financial goals in order of importance, and maintaining high awareness and control over your income and expenses. It all comes down to having the financial resources to allocate to the things that matter most to you. It's about clearing out clutter in your finances and belongings management.

It's crucial to remember that sticking to a minimalist budget does not always mean cutting costs. If an expensive object serves a meaningful function, you can still choose to own luxury products. A minimalist budget will probably motivate you to cut back on your spending. You will become more adept at allocating your finances towards what you truly want out of life rather than squandering them on unimportant items after you closely inventory your expenditures and set priorities for your objectives.

A minimalist budget can assist you in reorienting your spending towards experiences and goods that you truly value in life rather than things you buy merely because they are on sale. You won't overstuff your life with unimportant items, even while what you value might not be more affordable. For example, you might own a few high-quality pairs of shoes that you like and serve specific purposes in your life, rather than twenty pairs you acquired for a really good deal.

Being frugal with your finances and concentrating on the necessities is key to living on a minimalist budget. This sets it apart from being economical or frugal. A frugal individual uses coupons, seeks out the greatest offers, and accrues credit card points and incentives. It's admirable to shop around for the greatest price, but without a basic budget, it's still simple to overspend by purchasing items just because they're on sale. Here's where having a modest budget will come in handy. You may maximize your time and financial resources, set priorities for your goals, and refrain from impulsive purchases.

How Your Life Can Be Better on a Minimalist Budget

You can achieve simplicity and freedom by sticking to a minimalist budget. You can stop wasting money on unnecessary items by intentionally guiding your spending. In the short and long term, you can allocate your financial flow to what you truly want out of life.

Many people are caught in the never-ending cycle of earning and spending money. They simply wind up spending more money since they start seeking more upscale items if they put in the effort to earn more money. Their lack of awareness about where their money is going makes it difficult for them to "get ahead" in life, and they are never truly satisfied with what they currently have. It's quite simple to fall into the pattern that our society emphasizes acquisition as the path to pleasure.

You may end the acquisition cycle with a minimalist budget, which will also help you feel satisfied and in charge of your money (and your life). We still think like hunters and gatherers—we enjoy looking for things! In the modern world, this frequently manifests as shopping (sometimes aimlessly, just to see what's on sale or to find a good deal), perusing shopping catalogs, checking Craigslist or eBay, and engaging in other activities that entail merely looking for something to buy.

You can break yourself from the pattern of looking for something to buy, finding it, feeling regret or fulfillment for a little while, and then looking for something else to buy by adopting a minimalist budget. This cycle wastes time and money and doesn't make you happy. You know this deep down because even if you get thrilled searching for something to buy or anticipating a purchase, you don't feel delighted when you finally get it. You feel a little down, a little disappointed (and, in some cases, full-on regret!), even if it's something you've wanted for a long time! The only thing you can think of to cheer yourself up is to look for something else to buy next, maybe accessories for your recent purchase or just the next big thing.

However, living on a limited budget can help break the cycle of unnecessary purchases. It will show you how to achieve your goals and surround yourself with meaningful things that will make you happy. You can simplify your shopping, concentrate on acquiring only the items you truly need, and address the financial objectives that are most important to you by adhering to a minimalist budget.

Less stress is one of the main advantages of a minimalist budget. Thinking about bills or other responsibilities might be a never-ending challenge for some individuals. Paradoxically, these can be the same individuals who commonly buy things on impulse. The way that money is managed or not managed has a big impact on many relationships. One of the main causes of disagreements in relationships is money. Differing perspectives on entitlement and purchasing can strain relationships between parents and children (of all ages).

A basic budget can be useful in this situation. If you don't start managing your finances, they eventually take control of you and harm your relationships with other people. You may take charge of your financial situation by sticking to your minimalist budget. You can reduce wasteful spending to lower initial costs and eventually pay off your debt. You can make plans for the future that center on wise spending and enhancing your relationships and quality of life.

My Top 10 Easy Start Guide

You already know how to live a minimalistic lifestyle in all its forms. There are a tonne of additional factors that you need to think about in order to live a minimalist existence, and that will benefit you in the real world. While it is simple to declare in theory that one has sorted and simplified one's life and distanced oneself from things, this metamorphosis takes on quite a different appearance. Since it's not as simple as you may believe, the following advice, though, will make things a lot simpler.

1. the social media

Both material and information are abundant. Everybody uses social media.

However, upon closer inspection, we find that they also irritate us. Thus, consider cutting back on the amount of time you spend on social media. In addition to being drawn by likes on social media, boredom also draws many people in. These are all undesirable traits that take up a lot of our time. With that time, we could accomplish a lot more.

2. the Internet

You should attempt to live without the Internet if your job or other obligations do not require using your PC. Because excessive Internet browsing makes you less appreciative of the actual world. You'll see that your connection to reality is stronger without the Internet. You have a greater appreciation for them and are aware of what should be your priorities. We frequently check our mail, news, and the Internet excessively because we feel like we're missing something, and we're missing more of the real world now. Giving up or cutting back doesn't hurt, and the world will revolve even without the Internet. On the Internet, you miss more of the outside world than you do anything from the outside world on the Internet.

3. the desktop

These days, the desk is in the computer rather than the room. Because of this, the desktop should have the same orderly, spotless appearance as the previous desk. Organize your desktop in an hour; you won't need that long. These days, it's common to have endless documents and photos on your desktop, which gradually amass. Gaining a general understanding is beneficial, and using the computer once more will be more enjoyable. This holds on the desktop and for every aspect of life outside work. To ensure that tools and papers are always easily accessible, the workspace should be equally organized.

4. The TV

Things operate with televisions similarly to how they do with computers and the Internet. More often than not, boredom and concern motivate you to watch TV. The television is only for enjoyment, though. Don't you have enough entertainment in your lives? Does a square box have to entertain you? Decide consciously not to watch television. Without a TV, you might even find it more enjoyable, and you might even be able to cut it off from your gadget.

5. the mailbox

Everyone knows they have a full mailbox when they see so many useless letters and advertisements occupying it. And it might as well end now. All you need to do is place a sticker that reads "no advertising" on the mailbox. This tiny decal will spare you a great deal of anxiety. You do something nice for the environment, have more nerves, your inbox is more spacious, and you automatically avoid making needless purchases by taking advantage of the offers in the brochures.

6. Engaging in meditation

Additionally, minimalism entails enjoying oneself and spending more time with oneself. You want to search for and ultimately locate your inner center. You have less to cope with regarding material possessions, so you have more time to relax and meditate. It is up to you how, where, when, and how long you meditate. It is up to you to decide. You can get ideas from various apps and courses available on the Internet. You can maintain your inner balance by doing all of this.

7. nature

Because man is trapped in his never-ending rivalry, he grows further removed from the natural world. Considering that nature has, in a sense, raised mankind, it is somewhat depressing. "Less is more" is the maxim of minimalism, which heightens consciousness and fosters a closer bond with the natural world. You will discover that nature benefits you if you spend more time with yourself and less with pointless material possessions. Everyone can sense what I usually say—"nature is food for the soul"! Thus, you soon discover that most contemporary equipment, including computers, smartphones, and other gadgets, is excessive. Even if many believe otherwise, you don't need them to be content and happy. It's quite easy; sometimes, all it takes to sharpen the sense of the essential and recognize it is to connect with something natural.

8. your companions

One's buddies play a significant role in one's life. Our responsibilities and social media have altered communication in the modern day. However, does a friendship still exist when we send each other infrequent letters? For example, it can be minimalist if you focus on the essentials and return to your roots. You achieve this by getting together with your pals more frequently. Let's say you get coffee with an old friend.

9. Refuse and cancel.

Everybody occasionally has an appointment on his calendar that is, in reality, completely unneeded. Saying "no" is a distinct part of minimalism. You will feel that there is always something else you could have done with the time at every meeting you don't want to attend. For instance, you must lend a friend a little assistance. You say yes even if you have no other plans or time. It's a kind gesture, so that's all well and good, but if you don't like it, don't say yes either. Honesty with oneself and with other men is essential. Because every minute counts, focus only on the necessary things and don't waste them.

10. autonomous judgments

Your choice will also impact once you have chosen a minimalist lifestyle and focused on the necessities. People commonly answer yes, which leads to indecisive decision-making. But making a stand is important, particularly in minimalist living. You must express your attitude and make your argument. You must make brave choices and stick with them. Decisions are all that exist in life, and you will not succeed if you cannot make decisions.

The Effective Method For Organising Your Living Area

Starting with your living environment is the simplest way to incorporate minimalism. The most significant place in your life is your home, which should represent your identity and mental health.

You will experience a similar level of disarray and chaos if your home is overflowing. Rather, you should put effort into creating a clean and comfortable home.

You'll be able to relax when you get home thanks to this. Your home will appear messier and require more frequent cleaning when you have more possessions than is essential.

A minimalist house makes you feel more at ease, looks much better, and is easier to maintain. One way to get started is to go room by room through your house and declutter.

But whether it's your family or a flatmate, you must consider their requirements when you share a space. In situations like these, dialogue is essential, so sit and converse.

Inform them about your goals and the modifications you wish to make. Generally speaking, if you don't try to push your family to change, they will agree with you.

Make it a family activity to decide what is truly essential. Find out from everyone what they value and what they would be ready to give up to introduce some constructive minimalism into the home.

Let everyone consider how they would like to individually put it into practice. Reduce your time on activities that don't truly improve your mood, are ineffective, or waste your time.

Establish a time slot for decluttering so everyone can work on it together.

Like tidying up, chores should be divided evenly among all parties. You can be firm about this, but don't try to make someone start organizing their wardrobe simply because you are.

If they would like assistance, you can offer to help them tidy up their area, but don't suggest that it is required. The best way to influence people, especially children, is to set a good example.

When it comes to shared areas, consider what the other person needs or wants and remove everything unnecessary. If your housemates don't live like you do, try not to get upset with them.

Make your environment your own and incorporate minimalism into all you do, but don't impose it on others. You can talk to them about anything that's bothering you.

Speaking eases most problems that may emerge from allowing anger to fester. Avoid engaging in passive-aggressive behavior.

Try to be as open and sincere as you can. You might consider obtaining your apartment if they are a bad influence and don't assist you.

You can make a chore wheel to make sure that everyone in your family or housemates knows when it's their turn. Specify some guidelines that will be simple for everyone to abide by and justify their benefits to one another.

Make sure they don't think that everything is done to your advantage. You can help everyone comply with your basic requirements if you have a little patience and practice.

With time, you can strike the ideal balance between minimalism and your family. Be tough when requesting changes from people adamantly opposed to them, but let go of the minor details.

Practicing minimalism involves more than just tidying and arranging your home; it also involves changing your mindset.

To simplify decluttering each space, I have compiled a list of helpful tips. With little time, I will assist you with having a tidy, clutter-free, and organized home.

Chapter 3: 11–20 Days

Maybe you've realized this is easier than you anticipated, or maybe you're discovering it's tougher. As you appreciate a clutter-free house and accept the practice of getting rid of items you no longer need or want, you may experience conflicting emotions. Maybe you still feel guilty or remorse about getting rid of stuff you had a strong emotional tie to but no longer required or wanted. You are doing a fantastic job if you have reached the second leg of your challenge, regardless of how you feel. You should pause to acknowledge your accomplishments and the distance you have already covered. You're doing well.

We will go a little further for this section of the task. You'll thoroughly clean your homes and tackle more difficult jobs like removing stuff you've been holding onto "just in case." This may cause you to experience even more emotions, but if you keep going and follow each day as outlined, you will succeed greatly on your journey. Start on day 11 of your 30-day challenge if you're prepared to start the second leg. And never forget to be kind to yourself and take your time during this process. It is not just about organizing your house to live in a clutter-free space but also about introspection and personal growth.

Day Eleven

"Having less to do is now my goal, not getting more done."

- Francine Jay

If you are a family with small children, you will utilize today for two things; if not, you will use it for one. You will concentrate on the toy collection today if you are a parent of small children. You'll also concentrate on your valuable collections whether or not you have a family.

If this applies to you, we will begin by concentrating on the toys. Sort and arrange everything by going through each toy storage container. It is best to discard any broken toys. Donating toys that are no longer used is a good idea. Kids frequently have many toys, most of which they never play with. Giving your kids the gifts and toys they want is wonderful, but it often accumulates clutter in the house. While cleaning, consider a few toy-free activities you might encourage your kids to participate in. Instead, kids might go outdoors and pretend to play, assist with baking, or help with housework. In an earlier era, kids didn't have as many toys as they do now, but they managed to keep themselves busy without always needing the newest and greatest devices. It is good for your kids to do this since it helps them develop better time management skills and a stronger sense of imagination. It teaches kids how to take delight in life and prevents them from needing toys and other things to make them happy.

Searching through your collections was the second task. You might be keeping some of these collections because you've spent so much time and money on them. It's time to give them some serious thought and decide whether it would be worthwhile for you to keep them around. Naturally, it makes sense to preserve your collection if it makes you happy and is something you are proud of. If, on the other hand, it doesn't, and you just did it as a hobby, and you're not as happy with the collection as you once were, it could be time to part with it.

You are now prepared to tackle the everyday activities you will be sticking to during this challenge, having taken care of your toys and collections. Do your daily journaling, tidy one surface, and place one thing in the donation box. If it is getting full, you must take your donation box straight to the donation drop-off spot. Instead of storing it in the garage or elsewhere, just start a new one. Procrastination is why we frequently forget to bring them to the drop-off, which is just what we don't want.

Chapter 2: Living a Minimalist Lifestyle

Albert Einstein said, "Make things as simple as possible, but not simpler."

It's not a requirement of minimalism to own nothing. However, nothing ought to be yours. Joshua Becker is a minimalist writer.

How do you feel right now, on this particular day? What about yesterday? What are your plans for the future? Do you feel afraid or hopeful? In general, how content are you with every element of your life?

Permit me to ask you a few more questions now. Look inward and give a sincere response.

Examine Everyday Aspects

Do you find it difficult to find time for your family, yourself, and your hobbies? Are you constantly hustling and juggling multiple tasks at once?

Do you find it difficult to get to work every day? Do you rely on beer or sleeping medications to help you fall asleep at night after drinking coffee to stay awake during the day? Do you feel overburdened and under pressure?

Are you obliged to conduct or attend protracted, boring meetings that never seem to get anything done? Is your computer screen cluttered with folders that you take a long time to respond to requests for files from coworkers or your boss? Are your coworkers making fun of your office jungle because of the mess on your desk, cubicle, or room? Do you deal with so much paperwork that it prevents you from doing meaningful work? Do you gossip and have pointless conversations?

Do you wish you could work from home, relocate closer to your place of employment, or perhaps find a job close to where you live since you spend too much time driving or commuting to it?

Are you busy, but you still feel like you're stagnating? Are you feeling unmotivated? Do you think there is no purpose to life?

Do you have a lot of dirty dishes in your washbasin at home? Or is it possible that you are too busy to unload and have all of your cutlery in the dishwasher? Do you just keep piling up plates, cups, glasses, spoons, and forks in your dishwasher or sink until you run out of clean ones?

Have you ever had nothing to wear while you stood in front of your entire wardrobe? Do you spend many hours each day applying makeup and getting dressed up? Have you ever taken a long time to get ready or locate something to wear, which caused you to be late for work or an appointment?

Do you find hosting friends or unexpected guests difficult because your belongings are disorganized? Do you have trouble finding stuff in your room?

Does the mere thought of cleaning your home make you nervous? Are all of your chairs and tables cluttered? Is covering those tables and chairs with a beautiful blanket your notion of tidying up?

What state are your finances in? Do you make ends meet on a paycheck only? Are you having trouble keeping your finances under control? Are you drowning in debt, and do you have more coming in at an accelerated rate? Do you create a budget but fail to follow it? Do you swear to yourself when you set a budget, only to toss it out the window at the first sign of a sale? Do you believe using a credit card to make a purchase makes sense because you can always earn the money later on if you don't now have it?

Do you pay off loans, bills, and mortgages with a sizable portion of your income? Or does the upkeep of your home and/or car consume too much of your hard-earned money? Or do you have financial commitments to vices or addictions?

Do you have a project you intend to finish but have been putting off till later and later, until it becomes never? Do you frequently put off doing things because you're too preoccupied with work?

Do you want to work for yourself but think it would be awkward, challenging, and unaccepted in society? Even though you detest it, have you accepted that you will work for someone else until you are sixty?

Do you have to bring a lot of large luggage when you travel? Do you buy souvenirs throughout a significant portion of your vacation? When it's time to head home, do you have to pay for additional luggage to carry all those goodies and souvenirs?

Do you struggle to part with items that hold sentimental meaning for you? Or do you find it easy to let go, but do you feel empty or guilty as soon as you do?

I realize there are a lot of questions, but if you said "yes" to even one of them, you should be pleased that you have read this far in the book. Please continue reading. As the book continues, consider the questions that best capture who you are and how they could help you look more closely at that aspect of your life.

It's time to make life simpler. You must take back command of your time and assets. Now is the perfect moment to focus on the things that will bring you true happiness and contentment.

Advantages of Daily Minimalism

Examine the advantages of minimalism in your daily life to do this. By focusing more on developing your inner world, minimalism helps you break free from your addiction to material belongings.

It releases you from the shackles of consumer culture. It makes you value what you already have and yearn for more important things like your love, passion, mission, and life's purpose.

Evaluating Your Financial Condition

Like traveling, creating a budget is much easier when you know where and where you're going. You should know your financial situation before rushing to make a new budget. What is your monthly income total? How much money do you spend on necessities like food, housing, and transportation? What about desires for hobbies, entertainment, and eating out? Are there any costs you've forgotten about?

This chapter focuses on evaluating your financial situation so that you can plan your budget with knowledge. We'll walk through the essential processes of examining your sources of income, spending patterns, out-of-pocket expenses, and current debts. You must first have visibility into what is coming in and the precise location of every dollar at any given time. You can identify spending trends and areas of overspending in your new budget by keeping track of all your receipts and disbursements for one to two months.

After that, you may group your spending to see how much you spend each month on necessities vs wants. This aids in setting priorities for your budget's necessary expenses. Lastly, try to find ways to cut back on expenses, accelerate debt repayment, and begin saving. Knowing your entire financial baseline is crucial in creating a budget.

1.1 Monitoring Your Earnings and Outgoings

Monitoring your income and outflow for at least one to two months is the first and most crucial step in evaluating your financial situation. This offers insight into:

Your monthly net income (or income) after deducting taxes, necessary fixed costs for housing, utilities, insurance, and loans, and variable expenses for clothing, entertainment, food, and gas.

Irregular costs that come up every three months, every year, or occasionally

First, record every dollar coming in and going out using a spreadsheet, budgeting tool, or written ledger. Be thorough; keep track of everything, including your power bills, ATM withdrawals, and morning coffee. If you track every day for one to two months, you'll see reasonable spending patterns that you can adjust in your budget.

Sources of Income

Make a list of every reliable source of income you have. This could consist of Your net pay after deducting revenue from freelance work or side gigs, dividends on investments or income from rental properties, Social Security and other government support, and any other regular income.

To find out your overall monthly revenue, add up these consistent inflows. As a buffer, variable income such as bonuses or sporadic freelancing work might be entered separately.

Unchanged Costs

Next, record your fixed, non-negotiable costs, which remain the same for every billing cycle. Among them are:

Housing: taxes, insurance, upkeep costs, and rent or a mortgage

Paying off debts includes personal, auto, and education loans.

Health, life, house, and disability insurance

Utilities include garbage collection, cable, phone/internet, gas, water, and electricity.

subscriptions for software, newspapers, streaming services, and gyms

Transportation: automobile registration, passes for public transportation

Nursery and education fees

Child support, alimony, and any other fixed obligations

Documenting your monthly fixed expenses will assist in guaranteeing that your new budget gives them priority.

Changeable Costs

After that, start monitoring your daily variable spending, which varies. These consist of the following: groceries, takeaway and dining, petrol and fuel, tolls and public parking, ridesharing and taxis, amusement such as films and live performances, Bars, and alcohol. Buying: clothing, shoes, accessories, presents; Personal care: haircuts; products; Pet costs; ATM/cash withdrawals; and other daily or monthly expenses. Hobbies and recreational activities.

Monitoring variable costs helps you identify areas where you may optimize your spending.

One-time and sporadic costs

Lastly, make a note of any sporadic or one-time costs that come up from time to time. Examples include prescription drugs and medical bills, auto and home maintenance and repairs, veterinary expenditures, electronics purchases, training or classes, and professional services. Journey and getaway presents for holidays, birthdays, taxes, and annual or quarterly subscription payments.

Even though these are not monthly costs, factor them in to prevent unexpected costs from exceeding your budget. This comprehensive data, including all fixed, variable, and periodic expenses, will give you the visibility you need to create a realistic budget. The basis comes from closely monitoring spending for one to two months.

Chapter 6: Mindfulness Exercises

There are instances when your internal distractions force you to become unproductive for days rather than one. Unlike its physical equivalent, mental clutter didn't cost you anything. But even simply thinking about and attempting to control them has taken up much of your time. Additionally, they make you feel guilty, which may have led to you mistreating others around you or failing at your duties.

It simply makes sense to clear your mind. But this is not easy. An excessive number of thoughts can lead to mental congestion. You'll probably encounter this when you're overly busy or healing from a traumatic event. (If you're experiencing trauma, be sure to get help from a professional. Self-help may lead you to adopt inappropriate coping mechanisms, which can exacerbate your problem.)

It is quite beneficial to recognize mental clutter early on. Take a moment to stop when your thoughts wander or become sidetracked. Consider this: What was I meant to do this time? Go back to what you were doing. Although this could be a quick fix, it doesn't clear your mind of clutter. All it does is temporarily conceal them.

Create a mind map with the issues that are causing you mental and emotional distress to help you identify them more quickly. If you're the kind of person who does best under pressure, mental clutter might not be all that bad for you. Your overall attitude, nevertheless, would suggest otherwise. Regardless of your preference for or against pressure, being conscious of your bad feelings can inspire you to clear your mind.

Recognizing Strong Emotions

All emotions, whether they be pleasant or bad, have a purpose. Good feelings like joy, excitement, and thankfulness inspire you to do effectively. They may also act as motivation for you to carry out the actions you took to obtain them. On the other hand, unpleasant feelings like stress, worry, wrath, and fear should educate you on how to deal with or avoid the things that cause them.

Whenever you experience a powerful emotion, good or bad, consciously stop and take time for yourself. Recognize the feelings you are experiencing. Next, state the specific cause of it. Consider the possible consequences of every decision you make at this moment. Make no promises, swear, or hit. That will only result in losses, expenses, and more anxiety.

Understanding your bad emotions could help you understand why your life is so disorganized. Being aware of your feelings could help you gain more control. This will help you with your organizing endeavors.

Getting Rid of Illogical Thoughts

When decluttering, you can come across some items that make you question your purchasing decisions. Perhaps you loved the brand so much that you purchased an extra shirt. It's possible that you purchased an item because your friends and family do the same. Or perhaps you purchased it because the advertisements recommended it.

Those unreasonable ideas contribute to brain clutter. A single trigger can cause someone to act irrationally. They have a detrimental impact on your emotions and ability to make decisions. They are also known as thinking errors and cognitive distortions. You must recognize the type of thinking errors you're making in order to make corrections. The most common cognitive distortions and their fixes are listed here.

1. Excessive generalisation

You might believe differently, but one incident is simply one episode. When at least one comparable element appears in a different situation, you believe it will occur again. For example, if a close friend abruptly stopped seeing you or didn't say goodbye, you might start to believe that other people will follow suit. If a single child consistently bothers you, you could assume that's how all kids are. Concluding with too much detail could exacerbate your social anxiety.

Solution: Steer clear of the word "all" while concluding. In addition, you shouldn't state your conclusion as though you are positive. Additionally, use terms like might, could, and may. You can infer that some kids might also be that way if, for instance, one or a small number of them irritate you.

2. Labels and Inaccurate Labels

Overgeneralization and labeling are somewhat connected. In the two types of cognitive distortion, individuals are labeled or mislabeled—adding names or labels to oneself or others—based on insufficient evidence. Labeling occurs when you think of yourself as a bad person merely because you were not present at a family member's or friend's occasion. Regarding mislabeling, you presume someone is helpless if he doesn't give up on himself during a single conflict.

Solution: Give up using an action to characterize others and your personality. Ignoring adjectives and concentrating only on the verb is one way to accomplish this. For instance, a person just doesn't fight back if he doesn't fight back. Add no comments that contain derogatory terms like cowardly or weak.

3. Refinement

Your mind can discriminate between good and bad circumstances. When you focus only on the negative and neglect the positive, this becomes an issue. This screening casts you in question about your choices and your identity. For example, filtering makes you feel bad about making a single exam error rather than glad you got the answers right for every entry.

Solution:

Take out a piece of paper and a pen.

Put the event that set it off in writing.

Make a list of its advantages and disadvantages.

Positive things can occasionally need a visual reminder since your mind will not let them stay buried.

4. Undervaluing the Advantages

Filtering and this cognitive distortion are quite comparable. Here, you downplay or overlook any achievement or good thing that has happened. The distinction is that you do not choose to focus on bad circumstances. When you get promoted at work but still feel that you're not making progress in your life, that is an example of underestimating the positive.

Solution:

Accept things as they are and be grateful for the good things that did happen.

Refrain from beginning your description with "it's just."

For instance, don't say "it's just a promotion" if you receive one.

5. Dividing

Splitting occurs when you take into account only two extremes, such as win or lose, everything or nothing, etc. Other names for this type of cognitive distortion include dichotomous, polarised, black-and-white, and all-or-nothing thinking. Using terms and phrases like always, never, every time and all the time are examples of splitting.

Solution: Steer clear of absolute phrases, such as always, never, all, and nothing. Between black and white, there is a grey region. Between everything and nothing, there is something. Between winning and losing, there is a tie. Keep those in mind.

Getting Rid Of Your Inner Programming

It follows that whatever we are doing, we are doing it incorrectly if it is true that each of us is an editor of our reality. Most of us, if not all of us, would live life to the fullest if we were better editors of our reality. Simply put, we would be living to the fullest of our abilities.

The contrary is true, but you probably don't need me to tell you that. The majority of us fall well short of our greatest potential. What is happening? Why do we not use the power that every one of us possesses? How come the majority of us don't use this power if we can mold reality to fit our desires and personal narratives? It's not that hard to figure out. It boils down to just two terms: mind programming.

You have to realize that individuals in today's society are not naturally intelligent. We spread a wide variety of ideas among ourselves. The road is two-way. People can impact you in the same way that you can influence them.

We can all agree, though, that there is one enormous disseminator of influence that transcends all of these regional influences, which are frequently confined to your immediate social circle. The mass media and the economy are as follows.

Regretfully, economies driven by markets today have a purpose. It should come as no surprise that individuals in wealthy and developing nations have a very similar mentality. These typically originate from the same places.

For contemporary, market-driven economies to persist, certain fictions must endure.

In other words, if the world economy collapsed, it would be because people started prioritizing their needs over their wants when they woke up one day. Although it may sound alarmist or exaggerated, this is the whole truth. You quickly conclude that you don't need that much stuff if you're being totally honest with yourself.

When we talk about a need, we mean something you require to maintain the unity of your body and soul. We have a very narrow spectrum of demands if that's how we define it. We must have access to food and water, a roof over our heads, and a range of temperatures in which to live. Antibiotics and certain inputs that prevent or treat infections are also necessary; otherwise, not much else.

To be honest, there isn't much on this list that humans need to survive. Think about what would happen to the whole economy if everyone only cared for their needs. It would fall apart because certain fictions are necessary for the contemporary, globally market-driven economy to function.

It wants as many people to believe in these fictions as possible to flourish and grow. If not, everything would come to a complete stop. Simply put, the majority of the local and global economies would collapse if people only paid attention to what they truly needed.

For this reason, the system wants as many individuals as possible to internalize these fictions in addition to believing them. Put another way, people construct themselves and their narratives based on these concepts because they rely on them.

When new individuals who disagree with these viewpoints emerge, these individuals would join together, gesture, and declare, "You're out of line." You're strange. You're not normal. You are flawed in some way. See how this operates, do you? This concept has to spread because it has a life of its own. Because something can be "too big to fail," consider it akin to a mental infection.

This is enormous, and it keeps getting bigger every year. For it to survive, it must ensure that the following fictions are spread and that as many people as possible believe them. Individuals pass it on to their offspring, who in turn pass it on to their offspring, and so on. Furthermore, this system must remain intact by instituting various sanctions and incentives contingent on individuals' belief in them. It's a mental infection that spreads on its own.

These are only a few of the most popular myths this system frequently circulates and spreads. All of this is mental programming.

The Myth of Externally Driven Contentment

You can blame this myth if you find it difficult to be satisfied with anything, no matter how much money you produce or wealth you accumulate. This fiction just says you can never be the source of your happiness. All you are on this life trip is a passive passenger. Your happiness is based on factors outside of yourself.

These external items are what you aspire to and strive so hard for since they elevate your position and demonstrate your worth as a person. To achieve these goals, you must be willing to go above and beyond for whatever long and in whatever manner necessary. This may be how other people perceive you. It could be an item, a title, or an honor. Whatever the situation, it is external to you.

Contentment is an external state. It's not inside. This illusion holds that, no matter how much you may wish to believe otherwise, you can never truly be happy if there are things you are missing—things that, of course, change regularly.

How to Get Started

If minimalism is unfamiliar, you might be unsure where to start. The hardest aspect of starting along a new route is usually taking the first few steps, but the momentum keeps us going once we're moving. Anything is moving. So, make a plan before you take action.

What objectives do you have? What are your desires? Joy? Liberty? Knowledge?Love?Cash? Take a moment to consider your desires. Right now, where are you? What is the difference between where you are now and where you aspire to be? Well done if your life is already ideal for you! Most of us are behind you, but we intend to catch up with you eventually. What will it take to achieve where you want to go in life if you're not there yet? Minimalism may work as well for you as it has for me and countless others if you want more time, freedom, money, control over your life, and a simpler existence overall. You can live like Alexander Supertramp—a penniless minimalist who travels the rails, avoids bulls, and lives out of a backpack—it sounds fantastic! Alternately, you could be a wealthy minimalist, a billionaire in real estate or confections (sounds nice to me!), maybe with a raggedy old pick-up vehicle, frayed pants, and $20 Wal-Mart boots stained with leftover house paint.

You have a clearly defined Point A and a clearly defined Point B once you've determined where you want to be and evaluated where you are right now about your target. All that's left to do is sketch the line that joins them. The list will consist of several small tasks you need to complete to "get your ducks in a row."

Whenever possible, I prefer to work backward from Point B, the destination point. Richard Bach states, "you must begin by knowing that you have already arrived" in Jonathan Livingston Seagull. Usually, the hardest part is deciding to overcome all the obstacles to Point B. It might be unsettling to change. How do we weigh the benefits and hazards of changing course and possibly creating uncertainty against staying on the same, well-traveled paths? The good news is that you may easily return to a more intricate, demanding, and worldly existence at any point if you become a minimalist and find that you're not happy! Neither materialism nor minimalism has any sort of binding on you. Although there aren't many hazards, there could be limitless benefits.

Writing things down can be quite beneficial. Jot down a summary of your objectives, destination, or Point B. My dream job would be self-employment with lots of free time for writing, traveling, and putting my best value to use. to gain knowledge, develop, and genuinely meaningful love work, free from the burden of working 40+ hours a week just to make ends meet. To travel to a warm Spanish-speaking nation during the winter. To have enough time to learn about the world's biggest game, the stock market. To be content with my life and to live simply.

You can jot down brief thoughts and ideas as they occur or make a list or a brief paragraph. If you'd like, you can revise it afterward. Where are you right now, exactly? What is your main point? What must you do to join the line between Point A and Point B? Once more, working backward might be helpful in this situation. Try working backward if you can see where you are now and where you want to be, but you do not need to take all the steps to get there. I stated that I wished to work for myself, having lots of free time to write, travel, and concentrate on important projects. What action would you take right away to avoid all of that? Even though I wasn't sure, giving it some thought helped to clarify the entire process. If my GPS is malfunctioning and thick fog covers the entire road, how can I get to Point B? The step before reaching my point B, which is being self-employed and generally enjoying more financial and time freedom, must involve either running my own business or service or significantly increasing my income at my current job while working fewer hours (which is better but still not ideal or even realistic). So, what stage comes right before running a profitable business or service, assuming it's the penultimate step to achieving my goal? Supplying the public with something of great worth—something they desire or need—something that will amuse or assist them and make them laugh, cry, or smile. I would first need to determine what good, talent, or service I could provide to humanity that would uplift, amuse, or inspire people before I could take that next step.

I can start to see the path to my destination by thinking backward from Point B. In contrast, if I didn't work backward, I might never be able to envision or see the following step, leading to frustration and early surrender. I would give up when I couldn't see the way—I couldn't see how it was conceivable for me—rather than when I lacked the necessary perseverance or patience. Have you ever experienced that? Have you ever had the impression that you gave up on a desire or goal you had too quickly? It happens to all of us at some point, but the key is to keep going towards your objective until life presents an obstacle you can't overcome and feel that your desired outcome is feasible and realistic for you. Still, that is not common. Most of the time, people's inability to pursue their aspirations is due to their tendency to give up too quickly.

After going rearward from Point B, can you see the trail more clearly? Although achieving a goal like minimalism won't be easy, the good news is that after you push yourself past that initial hurdle, you'll be simplifying and improving your life.

Make a list of everything that comes to mind that you would need to do to get from point A to point B. It doesn't matter if you start at Point A or B, the end or the beginning. You will likely need to rearrange everything before your sequence of actions starts to take shape. This is a preliminary drawing of my list before my relocation to Arizona/California:

Create a strategy to save money.

Notify your family, friends, and landlord that I will be moving.

Invest in a more capable car that is newer and better for the trip.

Examine the area's cost of living, employment opportunities, and available housing.

Make a friend or friends who live nearby.

Invest in a reliable, current road atlas.

Determine my route in advance.

Purchase a mobile phone.

Reduce all I own so it will fit in my automobile.

Get my pet rat a cat carrier. Mia, when I'm traveling

Give me two weeks' notice at my job.

Before I go, stop by everyone.

Prepare sugar-rich roadside snacks, such as dates and bananas.

Go to the post office to pick up my mail.

I believe my initial list consisted of more than twenty or twenty-five items, but it was long ago, and I can't remember every detail. I had separate lists and pages of notes about how much money I would be able to save each week, about what I would have to throw away or give away, about what I could fit in my car, about friends and family I might be able to see on the way, about sights to see along the long I-40 as I headed west, about job leads, and about potential places to live in both Arizona and California. I must have had lists and notes on twenty or thirty pages. I prepared and planned for almost the full year. Taking up a pen and some paper and putting everything down was the first step; living and working in Arizona or California was the last.

You may start creating your blueprints or your road plan to get there if you have a clear idea of where you want to go and where you are right now concerning your objectives. Divide your map into manageable steps, then take each step step-by-step. Step forward, and don't turn around. Aim for your goals and note how much closer you got to them with each step you took. Also, take a moment to reflect on how you felt while taking that step. You'll probably be inspired to continue moving in that direction if you notice even a small improvement. Start with something basic.

www.ingramcontent.com/pod-product-compliance
Lightning Source LLC
Chambersburg PA
CBHW052137110526
44591CB00012B/1765